Treat, Treat, and Move Your Feet Spiritual Mind Treatment Workshop

What it is, and how to use it to raise one's consciousness

RESOURCE BOOK
&
WORK BOOK

By

David W. Sharer, RScP

ISBN: 1448682819
ISBN 13: 9781448682812

Treat, Treat and Move Your Feet
Spiritual Mind Treatment
Workshop
Table of Contents

Page

Acknowledgements_____1

Introduction_ _____2

1. Spiritual Mind Treatment

• What is Spiritual Mind Treatment_____6

• What is the Purpose of Treatment_____9

• What Are the Methods of Treatment?_____9

2. What do we believe?

• Explain the Top Core Principles_____11

• Describe the Creative Process_____21

• Mental Equivalents_____23

• Treat, Treat and Move Your Feet_____27

• Practicing the Presence _____29

• Forgiveness_____31

• Gratitude_____31

3. How Does Spiritual Mind Treatment Work?____ 33

4. Basis For Spiritual Mind Treatment _____35

5. How to Give a Spiritual Mind Treatment_____41

6. Figure 1, Metaphysical Symbol_____54

7. Figure 2, Graphic Picture of Treatment Process. _____ 55

8. Figure 3, Spiritual Mind Treatment Practice Worksheet_____56

9. Affirmations_____60

10. Experiential #1-9_____75

11. Bibliography_____89

Treat, Treat, and Move Your Feet

Acknowledgements

I am grateful for my Practitioner and teacher, Dr. Betty Henderson RScP, for her inspiration and encouragement in the preparation of this book and the resultant workshop.

Diane Gesell, RScP, Steve Higgins, RScP, Vickie Estrella, Ruth Dalton, Sally Kasner, RScP, Ken Kasner, RScP, Hazel Bowman, Nancy Young, RScP, Glen Copeland, Betty Henderson, RScP, Midge Read, Paul Myers, Elin Myers, Linda Niles, Deanna Gerard, Penny Hershman, Patricia Weiberg, and Sue Sharer, RScP, who attended my first Spiritual Mind Treatment work shop, I am grateful for their support of this work and their encouragement to have it published. Their comments lead to revisions and improvement in the book itself.

I am eternally grateful to JoDee Vale for her expertise in publishing. JoDee took my 8 x 11 draft and formatted it for publication; she developed the book cover, and coordinated with the Publisher, and sent it to them for publication. She has truly been a great help in getting this book published.

Last, but not least, I am thankful for my wife Sue, who supported me in this work "

1

**Spiritual Mind Treatment
Workshop**

Introduction

A major part of my spiritual practice is doing Spiritual Mind Treatments for myself and others. A student of Religious Science gets introduced to Spiritual Mind Treatment in the accredited Foundation Class. This is the first class, and a prerequisite for all future accredited class work. The minister often talks about treatment during the Sunday message and in fact does a treatment during the service each Sunday for all those named in the Prayer Chest and those mentioned by congregants during the service.

Ernest Holmes gave us, in his teaching, method of affirmative prayer which we call Spiritual Mind Treatment. This method is unique to all other new thought teachings. In my opinion, Spiritual Mind Treatment is one of the greatest processes Ernest gave to all of us who study the Science of Mind.

Spiritual Mind Treatment is an affirmation of the Divine Presence in and through all things, all people, and all events. Ernest Holmes says that whenever we identify our thinking with some person or thing, we identify him or her or it as the object of that thinking, and automatically, because there is only One Law operating, the result of our treatment or prayer is in the One Mind. The mere act of identifying our affirmation with that person or thing brings about an effect upon him, her, or it.

The reality is that whatever we put our attention to in our thinking process is, in fact, a form of treatment in that the word or thoughts of the one doing the thinking goes into the subconscious mind, which immediately goes to work to produce those thoughts into form.

While many congregants take class work which involves learning how to do treatment work, there are many who do not. It is for those who do not take class work (and even many who have) that this workbook is intended to help on their Spiritual Path.

This workbook will identify the difference between prayer as taught in traditional churches and Spiritual Mind Treatment as taught by Religious Science. It also describes the purpose of Treatment, and identifies the various methods of Treatment.

Before getting into actual treatment work, the workbook will review what we believe. We'll discuss the Top Ten Core Concepts as taught by Ernest Holmes, Mental

3

Equivalents, Forgiveness, the Creative Process, and what it means to "Practice the Presence".

After going over this information, the workbook will explore how treatment works and many of the Principles associated with a truly powerful and successful treatment. This is under the heading of the basis for Spiritual Mind Treatment.

The second half of the workbook will focus on how to do a Spiritual Mind Treatment, using the Five Step Argumentative method, as taught by United Centers for Spiritual Living. In this phase there are many examples of Treatment for specific desires of the one doing the treatment. Each step of treatment and the purpose behind each step is identified giving the student many examples for each. This will reinforce the knowing that Spiritual Mind Treatment should be given with deep feeling and belief that the work has already been done. At the end of this workbook are nine experientials; these exercises are intended to give the student the tools to do Spiritual Mind Treatments for themselves and others. Also, these exercises will enable the student to develop the feelings necessary for a successful demonstration of their desire.

Ernest Holmes stated "through the use of faith, and belief in affirmative prayer, which we call spiritual mind treatment, something greater than ourselves acts upon us. If we had the same faith in spiritual laws that we have in physical ones, our faith would be complete and miracles would happen every day. As we turn to the Divine Center within us, then, realizing the fullness of the activity of the living Spirit is working through us, let us announce our good, without effort or strain, and in a relaxed receptivity, let us know that the Law of Mind acts upon our word. Not asking how or why, but with simple acceptance and complete belief, let us permit this good to be established in our experience."[1] This is the very essence of treatment work. One must have the faith and belief in the very power of their word.

---

[1] Science of Mind Text Book, page 165, Ernest Holmes

5

What is Spiritual Mind Treatment?

Spiritual Mind Treatment is affirmative prayer, spoken in a scientific manner, in faith and with conviction. It is the alignment of our thought with the perfect right action of God.

Treatment is "the art, the act, and the science of consciously inducing thought within the Universal Subjectivity, for the purpose of demonstrating that we are surrounded by a Creative Medium which responds to us through a law of correspondence. In its more simple meaning, treatment is the time, process and method necessary to the changing of our thought. Treatment is clearing the thought of negation, of doubt, and fear, and causing it to perceive the ever-presence of God."[2]

"Spiritual Mind Treatment is the same as prayer; if the prayer is recognition of Spirit's Omniscience, Omnipotence, and Omnipresence, and a realization of man's unity with Spirit. If on the other hand, one is holding to the viewpoint that God is some far off Being, whom he would approach with doubt in his thought, wondering if by some good luck he may be able to placate God or persuade Him of the wisdom of one's request--then, there is little similarity between prayer and

---

[2]   Science of Mind Text Book, Glossary, Ernest Holmes

treatment."[3]

"Prayer is Communion. It is attention. To "Be Still, to quiet the mind to outer activities;" to know that the Divine Presence is All There Is. To submerge one's self in this Oneness—this Allness—we completely surrender our mind, body and affairs to this Love. We sense, feel and respond to Reality."[4]

"Spiritual Mind Treatment is specific use of thought for definite purposes."[5]   "A treatment is a conscious movement of thought, and the work begins and ends in the thought of the one giving the treatment."[6]

A treatment is a spiritual entity in the mental world and is equipped with power and volition—as much power and volition as there is faith in it, given to it by the mind of the one using it—and operation through the Law. This is the Law of Cause and Effect.

Prayer in its truest sense is not a petition, not a supplication, not a wail of despair; rather it is an alignment, a unifying process which takes place in the

[3]   Science of Mind Text Book, page 149, Ernest Holmes
[4]   The Joy of Being, Dr Vetura Papke, page 60
[5]   Ibid, page 63
[6]   Science of Mind Text Book, page 171, Ernest Holmes

mind as it reaches to its Divine Self and to that Power which is greater than human understanding.[7]

Prayer is communion with the Unity of all life. And this communion pronounces life to be Good. In this act of communion the individual becomes co-partner with the Eternal and gives birth to time, space and conditions.[8]

Scientific mental healing is...a systematic process of reasoning which unearths the mental cause or idea underlying disease, and presents the Truth about man's being.[9]

---

[7] The Essential Ernest Holmes. Page 37, Edited by Rev. Jesse Jennings

[8] Ibid, page 38

[9] The Science of Mind, pg 203.

What is the Purpose of Treatment?

The purpose of Treatment is to change one's experience through an intelligent, definite method which has its basis in scientific principles.

"Mental or Spiritual treatment should bring into actual manifestation the health and happiness which are mankind's normal and divine heritage. This healing power is a consciousness of the Unity of all Life and the spiritual nature of all being."[10]

When doing treatment work we know that the experience must be in our consciousness. When we change our consciousness, the false condition will disappear. "Change your thinking, change your experience."

What Are the Methods of Treatment?

There are two distinct methods; one is called argumentative, and the other realization.

---

[10]   The Science of Mind, pg 164

a. <u>**Argumentative Method.**</u>

This is a process of mental reasoning in which the one doing the treatment argues to himself about the truth in this situation. He presents a logical argument to Universal Mind, or Principle, and if it carries with it complete evidence in favor of a positive outcome, the situation should be healed.

1. "His word, operative through Universal Mind, sets a law in motion, on the   subjective side of life, which objectifies through the body as healing."[11]

b. <u>**Realization Method.**</u>

"The realization method is one whereby the one doing the treatment realizes within him/herself—without the necessity of step by step building up a conclusion—the perfect state of the patient."[12]

---

[11]   The Science of Mind, Ernest Holmes page 171
[12]   Ibid, page 171

What do we believe?

To discuss what we believe about the spiritual principles and the creative process, the Top Ten Core Concepts as taught by Ernest Holmes, are an excellent starting point, leading to healing through Spiritual Principles.

Core Concept One is "God is all there Is". From this one infinite source flows the spiritual, mental, and physical Universe—all Life, all Love, all physical form or effect, all Creation, all Physical and Spiritual Principles and Laws are contained within the One. Each human being is a creation of God, made of the God-substance, a unique, individualized incarnation of Spirit. This incarnated Spirit is the essence of every human being.

All physical and spiritual Principles and Laws are contained within the One. Because each of us is an incarnation of the One Spirit, all life is inseparably One. There is a Divine Wholeness, a total interconnectedness at the Source. This Oneness is irrevocable and eternal. It is WHO I AM. All humans are One with God, One with each other, and One with all Life, animate and inanimate.[13]

---

[13]   Science of Mind, text book pp 63-80

There is not a place where God is not. God is everywhere present with all of Its attributes.

God is All Intelligence. God is All Power; God is the Source behind all Its creation. God is Love and Law continually expressing Itself throughout Its creation.[14]

Core Concept Two describes the Triune nature of being within the One: Spirit, Soul, and Body. This is God as macrocosm. God as Spirit is Universal Mind in the conscious mode. God as Soul is Universal Mind in the subjective mode. It is also called the Law or the Creative Medium and has no volition of its own. It manifests impersonally the directives implanted by Spirit as God as Body in the physical Universe and all the forms it contains—all the visible manifestations of invisible Cause. Body or form is always an effect. Each human is a projection of God in microcosm, thus is endowed with the triune nature of God, and expresses that nature in all three aspects, or modes of his/her being. My conscious mind is Universal Spirit individualized in me as my spirit. My subjective mind performs within me all the roles of the Universal Subjective in the Cosmos. I am an individualized expression of God at the point of my conscious perception. My physical body is the vehicle through which I function in the physical universe. With

---

[14]   Living the Science of Mind, pp. 1-14, 56-57

my human senses and emotions, I experience the events and conditions of my world of affairs. *All experiences are effects and subject to change.*

Core Concept Three states that Spirit is the great causative power of the Universe. The Word, or thought, of God eternally initiates the divine creative process. In this process, Law is continuously set in motion to create, from the Unformed Substance, innumerable forms which follow the thought-patterns of Spirit. One Power alone really acts. This Power is the Word of Spirit, God, or Universal Conscious Intelligence. The human spirit is one with Universal Spirit, and human thought is creative and re-enacts in microcosm the Divine Creative Process. According to my thinking and beliefs, I co-create the conditions of my life. The master teacher said "It is done unto you as you believe." The Universe can give me only the good that I consciously accept. My thought tends to reproduce in my experience a reflection of the consciousness behind it. My thinking brings about a change in my experience. All change can occur, however, only in accordance with my acceptance and embodiment of the Truth.

Core Concept Four states the Infinite Nature of God, all conceivable Good, is eternally available and ready to flow into human experience. This flow of Good is activated and/or increased by human belief, faith, and acceptance, resulting in physical demonstration. The expression of this essential belief, faith, and acceptance is prayer (Spiritual Mind Treatment). The human re-enactment of the cosmic creative process happens naturally. In this process, prayer, or spiritual mind treatment is one effective way to increase our belief in and acceptance of the Universal Good. The techniques of treatment assist in clarifying the thoughts, true desires, and the awareness of the one doing the prayer, of the process that is taking place. The process works through the Law of Cause and Effect. "As you sow shall you reap." Whatever thoughts you place into the Universal Mind will tend to return to you in manifested form. *Remember whatever you perceive, you will receive; where attention goes, energy flows.*

Prayer is a power when it reveals that the one praying is in alignment with Universal Harmony, consciously recognizing Spiritual Truth that has always existed.

Core Concept Five "This is a Universe of Wholeness, Allness, Oneness. Spirit is a transcendent, perfect whole, that, in Its Infinite Inclusivity, harmoniously embraces all

14

seeming opposites". Each human being is endowed with free will and can thus choose to experience freedom or bondage, abundance or lack, joy or misery, all of which lie within the Infinite Inclusivity of God. We are not punished for our mistakes of ignorance or negative behavior. However, we do experience, through the impersonal action of the Law, the consequences of the choices we have made.

You get what you think about (positive and negative). All forms of matter and energy are attracted to a like vibration. What you think about, you bring about. Energy attracts like energy; everything draws to itself that which is like itself. This is called the Law of Attraction.

The Law of Attraction is one of the most powerful and life altering forces in the universe, one of the necessary components of affirmative prayer, and is a key to living a conscious life.

If we have a feeling of desire in our consciousness when we pray about something, the law of attraction matches that feeling by giving a greater feeling of desire, instead of the thing you are praying for. When we pray affirmatively for a desired outcome, we must be clear to have an attitude and feeling nature of already experiencing the desired outcome and allow the Law of

Attraction to match our belief.

A dictionary definition of perfect is: "lacking nothing essential to the whole; complete of its nature or kind."

Because my nature is a projection of God's nature, I have the freedom to choose my own thoughts and follow my own path. <u>With this freedom I am accountable for the outcomes of the choices I make.</u>

This concept of the Higher Power as a single Principle, an inseparable Wholeness, corresponds to Unity of all life. There is only one power and that is God, and that power is perfect, that power is my power Now. When we come into alignment with our Source and universal harmony we recognize the perfection of All There Is.

Core Concept Six states that the Universe is of infinite abundance, spiritual, mental, and physical. This Bounty of Spirit, this Allness of Good, is limitless and can never be exhausted or depleted. This infinite bounty of Spirit is the birthright of every human. This boundless supply of Good is our inheritance, now and forever, but we can experience any form of it only to the degree that we <u>believe</u> it is ours, <u>accept it</u>, <u>claim it</u>, and <u>embody</u> it. The word embody is defined as to give a body to a spirit; to make concrete and perceptible, to cause to become a

16

body or part of a body."[15]

I can experience this infinite abundance in my life as love, money, health, talent, fulfillment, or any other form of earthly riches that my mind can conceive. The kind of abundance and the amount of it that I can have is the kind and amount that I can conceive and embody.

There is a limitless supply of everything. God is the Source behind all abundance, not the job or any other thing outside us. It is within us and all around us at all time. It is omnipresent.

Core Concept Seven says this is a reciprocal Universe. For every visible form, there is an invisible counterpart. Everything in nature tends to equalize itself, to keep its balance true. Human life demonstrates the reciprocal nature of the Universe in the Laws of Attraction, Mental Equivalents, doing and being done by, and other such principles. Holmes in the Science of Mind textbook describes the principle of reciprocity as "The general law that what we are to the Universe, the Universe will be to us; that what we give out; that we shall receive back; that like attracts like; that "whatsoever a man soweth, that shall he also reap; and that no man escapes the Law." Whatever we perceive we will receive. Wherever attention goes, energy flows.

---

[15] Merriam Webster's Collegiate Dictionary

If I habitually live with thoughts of poverty, failure, loneliness, helplessness, illness—then such conditions tend to manifest in my life. If I habitually live with thoughts of love, compassion, joy, peace, achievement, and abundance—then such conditions tend to manifest in my life.

Within Universal Harmony, the Divine Givingness must always be balanced by equal acceptance.

Core Concept Eight states The Universe exists in the Eternal Now, each moment complete and perfect within itself. There can be no place for divine anger, unforgiveness, or punishment. Human forgiveness is the process that frees us to live in the Eternal Now. It is essential that we wholly forgive ourselves and all others before real spiritual growth can flourish. Unforgiveness, or holding resentment is a misuse of Spiritual Law, a rejection of the Oneness of all Life.

Holmes says, "Neither the consciousness of Spirit nor the laws of the Universe hold anything against us; wherever we turn to them in recognition and acceptance, they immediately flow through us, imparting the Divine Givingness…"

Core Concept Nine states that Immortality is a Universal Principle. God knows only Life. Death is a human concept. The very essence of every human is the incarnation of God at the center of his/her being.

Immortality means the eternal continuance and self knowingness of my individualized consciousness, forever expanding as I grow in enlightenment and the capacity to love.

There is, within myself, an irrefutable recognition that the present experience is only one spiral of an eternal journey toward the light.

All men are incarnations of God and the soul can no more be lost than God can be lost. Each of us is an individualized expression of the Divine. As God cannot die, neither can we.

Core Concept Ten describes the Cosmic Christ as not a person, but a Universal Presence...the Universal image of God present in all creation. Each human partakes of the Christ nature to the degree that the Cosmic Christ is recognized and revealed through him or her. To that degree, he/she becomes the Christ.

The Christ Consciousness is truly the "pattern that

connects," the seamless garment that enfolds all life as One.

We must understand the Christ is not a person but a Principle. It was impossible for Jesus not to have become the Christ, as the human gave way to the Divine, as the man gave way to God, as the flesh gave way to Spirit, as the will of division gave way to the will of unity —Jesus the man became a living embodiment of the Christ.[16]

The life of Jesus portrays the spiritual evolution of each of us as we are on the path of unfolding. The unfolding begins with the immersion of each of us into a stream of Life, Christ Consciousness, realizing there is no life apart from Universal Spirit and recognizing it as our point of origin. We are all the offspring of Spirit or the Creative Mind, and at some level we realize that we are a part of Infinite Being. When we embody the Christ Mind, we have the ability to be the savior of our own consciousness.

From the ten Core Concepts we learn that God is All there is; the Triune Nature of God is Spirit, Soul and Body; the Creative process; and affirmative prayer (Spiritual Mind Treatment). We also learn that each of us

---

[16]   The Essential Ernest Holmes, pg 192

is an individualized expression of the Divine and that Spirit resides within us. "We are individual points in the Consciousness of God or the original Creative Spirit of the Universe. We are points where It thinks through us, as us, or, as we say, God as man in man is man." [17]

Creative Process

The creative process is easily understood by reviewing the Metaphysical Chart in Figure I (Page 23). In the Top section is Universal Spirit, Love, Absolute, First Cause, and Conscious Mind. The center section is Universal Subjective Mind, Soul, Law, and Creative Medium by which Spirit passes into form. The lower section is the physical manifestation of Spirit—form, effects, or conditions. The creative process is that Spirit speaks Its word into the Universal Subjective Mind which goes to work to produce the correlation into physical form.

Since each of us is an individualized expression of the One, we have the triune nature of the Divine within us. We create our experience by our thoughts and emotions and the beliefs behind them. "We must remember that the Law of Mind, or Spirit, which we may use consciously, will always return to us exactly what we are thinking." Further, "the Law of Mind is a Law of

---

[17]   Living the Science of Mind, pg 152

Reflection returning to us the exact content of our thought." The Law is not a physical law. It is of Mind and Spirit. It is a Law which responds to our word-- that is, our thought, mental image or idea. The creative nature of our thought involves the sum total of the content of our mind. "Our habitual thought patterns are being reflected in all our images of thought".[18] If we do not like what we are experiencing, we can change our thinking and we'll change our experience. Change your thinking, change your experience. The Law reflects back to us our consciousness. If we want to know where our consciousness is, we look at our life which is the perfect reflection of the sum of our consciousness.

"The Law of Mind works as a law of identity, reproducing identically the content of our thought in and as our experience. It works by involution and evolution. Involution is defined as invoking the Law, setting the Law in motion, giving a spiritual mind treatment. We must get the ideas into the mind and allow them to work out".[19]

"We are surrounded by an infinite Law that can do anything. There is no limit to It and It does not know anything about big and little. But what the Law does for

---

[18] Effective Prayer, pg 119
[19] Can We Talk To God? Ernest Holmes pg 125

<u>us It must do through us.</u>   "We must consciously and subjectively accept only that which we wish to experience". Mary Baker Eddy says "Stand guard at the portal of your mind". "The one who successfully uses spiritual mind treatment is merely one who knows these things, practices them, and understands and believes them".[20]

It is very important when doing Spiritual Mind Treatment that the one doing the treatment unifies him/herself with the source of creation (All There Is). Recognizing that the One Perfect Life flows through us is the highest form of healing.

The creative process is a state of giving thought to what you want with such clarity that your Inner Being responds by offering confirming emotion or feelings. We all use the creative power every time we think and use our own mind. Remember there is only One Mind and our individual mind is using it to create our experience.

Mental Equivalents

How much life can any man experience? "As much as he can embody."[21] This is called Mental Equivalents. "If our

---

[20]   Living the Science of Mind, pg 178, Ernest Homes
[21]   Science of Mind Text Book, pg 280, Ernest Holmes

belief is limited, only a little can come to us, because that is as we believe."[22] "Anything that you want in your life —a healthy body, a satisfactory vocation, friends, opportunities, and above all the understanding of God— you must furnish a mental equivalent of what you desire."[23] One should remember that the thing you see in the outer is the precipitation on the physical plane of a mental equivalent held by one or more people."[24] The secret of successful living is to build up the mental equivalent that you want; and to get rid of the mental equivalent you do not want. It is a fact that we always demonstrate our consciousness; you demonstrate what you habitually have in your mind. You experience in the outer what you really think in the inner. If you want to be healthier, happier, younger, more prosperous, above all, if you want to get nearer to God—you must change your thought and keep it changed.

"To change your thought and keep it changed is the way to build a new mental equivalent."[25] Think of the conditions you want to produce. If you want to be happy, healthy, prosperous, doing constructive work, having a continuous understanding of God, you think it, feel it and

---

[22] Science of Mind Text Book, pg 280
[23] The Mental Equivalent, pg 5, Emmet Fox
[24] Ibid, pg 7
[25] Ibid, pg 24

get interested in it. True feeling in thought is interest.

Mental Equivalent is having a subjective idea of the desired experience. As we bring ourselves to a greater vision than the range of our present concepts, we can then induce a greater concept and therefore demonstrate more in our experience. One way of increasing your mental equivalent is to visualize what you desire as already yours, see it, feel it, know it is already done. Then it will manifest into form. One can increase his/her Mental Equivalent through continual practice of doing treatment work.

While it is true that, so far as Principle is concerned, we can have what good we desire according to the Law of Cause and Effect, it is also true that no matter what we may desire we shall only have what we are able to accept. Since this accepting is mental, we shall only experience what we are able to embody in our thought. Each one will automatically attract good into his experience in accord with his acceptance of Life. This is one of the principal ideas of the Science of Mind and is called the Law of Mental Equivalents.[26] Every demonstration is made at the exact level of the expectancy, the expectancy embodied in thought.[27]

---

[26]   The Essential Ernest Holmes, pg 41
[27]   Ibid, pg 41

Treat, Treat, and Move Your Feet

Treat, Treat, and Move Your Feet means to know that what you are treating for is already yours in the present moment. One technique I use in my treatment work is to visualize what it is I desire. Seeing myself having whatever I desire and enjoying it in the moment is an effective way of building a mental equivalent, enabling the demonstration of what I desire to manifest in my life experience. If you want to be healthier, happier, younger, more prosperous, visualize yourself as already being that desire. An example if you want to experience greater health in your life, see yourself as perfect health, trust, in faith, that you already have health and you will demonstrate it. If it is for a job, see and act as though you already have the job. Get up each morning as through you were going to work, dress accordingly for the job. And see yourself as employed, in the right job and at the right salary Now. If the job you are seeking requires different skills than you currently have, then take whatever action you can to acquire the necessary skills, such as going back to school When seeking more supply see yourself as having all your needs being met with plenty of money to spend and plenty to share with your fellowman. Also, associate with prosperous people.

26

Whatever you treat for, believe that you already have the resultant demonstration. <u>Remember you must change your thought and keep it changed</u>. The above action on your part is another tool to change the conditions in your life. If you want to be happy, healthy, prosperous, doing constructive work, having a continuous understanding of God, you think it, feel it and get interested in it. True feeling in thought is important in demonstrating a change in life experience.

Meditate and treat on your desire and take whatever action is revealed to you to change your beliefs which will lead to the physical manifestation of your desired good.

<u>You must recognize that you do not do the healing</u>: <u>God does the healing.</u> The MIND is the Actor and you are the director. When you release your treatment into the Law you must know that the work is already done and trust the creative process by letting go and letting God. As Emerson said "get your bloated nothingness out of the way."

Eric Butterworth, in his work entitled Unity of All Life, says "Identify yourself with abundance, claim abundance. Wherever you see affluence, say to yourself, I am one with that. Begin to act as if success and prosperity are yours and that it is impossible for you to fail. Accustom yourself to thinking that you are surrounded by a divine presence that wishes you only good because you are an organ of its activity."

Practice the Presence

The master teacher, Jesus, said that "Seek ye first the Kingdom of God and all things will be added unto you." This means seeing God in everything and everyone at all times. In Religious Science we are taught that God is All There Is and all living things are but an individualized expression of the One. Each of us acts as a conduit through which God expresses Itself through us as us. We know that God is within and surrounds everyone and everything, and we experience life according to our beliefs and the emotions we hold behind those beliefs.

God is perfect, whole, and complete and is the source behind all Its creation; God is love, harmony and total goodness. God knows nothing about disease, fear, hate or other negative emotions. It only knows Itself, which is total goodness. Putting your attention on the Divine is the greatest of all healing practices. Practicing the Presence of God is a great way to raise your consciousness to a higher level.

28

Our life experience is the direct result of our consciousness. Through our ego, we tend to feel separate from our Source. When we buy into the race consciousness (all thoughts and ideas ever thought by human kind), we feel separate from our Source; we will always experience those thoughts and beliefs that we put our attention to. If we get caught up in the evening news and dwell upon those things we do not want in our life experience, they will tend to be our experience. To change our belief and experience we need only discover the blocking belief and change it with a unifying one to initiate a new Cause which the Law will then produce into form. Change your thinking, change your life.

To Practice the Presence of God is to awaken within us the Christ Consciousness.[28]

---

[28]   The Science of Mind, page 413.

Forgiveness

It is only when we have completely forgiven others and ourselves that we can get clearance in our own minds, for we are judged by the judgment with which we judge. If we criticize, condemn, and censure, these are the attitudes that occupy our thinking. They will not only reflect themselves outwardly, they will also reflect themselves inwardly. They must do this, for the without is merely an extension of the within, and the within is the determiner of that extension. If we want a complete clearance of our attitudes, we must forgive everything and everyone. Whether we like it or not or whether we accept it or not, this is one of the great truths of life.

Not only should we forgive others but we should equally forgive ourselves. Until we release all of our own previous mistakes and failures, pain and suffering, we shall merely be monotonously repeating them today.

Gratitude

Gratitude is the gift of being thankful. The act of expressing gratitude is the door to the abundance of God and all creation. It is a love vibration. When we are grateful we exude a feeling tone of acceptance and appreciation. Thanksgiving allows us to connect to what we are experiencing from the heart space within. It is when we move our heads to our hearts that we open up to the sacred in all things and allow ourselves to feel a sense of oneness with all life. By being grateful we become aware of the presence of God in all.

When you have an attitude of gratitude, you put yourself in acceptance of what is happening at the present moment, without judgment. In that state we know that the Presence of the Divine is in all things right now. Being thankful for what will be before we actually experience it grants us the consciousness to receive that which we desire. An attitude of gratitude is a key element in moving us to a state of receptivity. We then can let go and let God bring about our desired outcome.[29]

The attitude of thanksgiving and practicing gratitude carries us beyond the field of doubt into one of perfect faith, acceptance, receptivity and realization. By being thankful and grateful we attract the hidden potentialities of life.

I recommend that everyone start a gratitude journal. At the end of each day write in your journal everything you are grateful for. Make this a part of your spiritual practice by doing it each and every day.

[29]   5 Gifts for an Abundant Life, Diane Harmony, pg 21

31

How Does Spiritual Mind Treatment Work?

Spiritual Mind Treatment works by setting the subjective Law in motion by inducing right concepts on the subjective side of life. First we recognize the Oneness of all there is. We then unify with it; we then reveal the Truth about the condition we desire to change; we give thanks and then release our word into the Law, knowing the works already done, we let go and let God.

The key to a powerful treatment is recognizing the Unity of all life with the One Creative Source behind all Creation and believing, with feeling, that you already have the thing you desire.

The human spirit is one with Universal Spirit; All There Is, and the human subjective merges with the Universal Subjective. All human thought is creative and re-enacts in the Divine Creative Process. Through our conscious thinking and our subjective beliefs, we re-enact in microcosm the continuum of creation. According to our thinking and beliefs, we co-create the conditions of our life. Our thought tends to reproduce in our experience a reflection of the consciousness behind it. A change in consciousness and thinking will result in a change to our experience. Life externalizes at the level of our thought.[30]

---

[30]   The Essential Ernest Holmes, pg 15

The Law is Universal Subjectivity, the Creative Medium, Soul and the Potentiality of all things. The Universal Creative Medium is a receptive and plastic medium which surrounds us on all sides, which permeates and flows through us. When we think, we think upon It, since it is Omnipresent. The creative medium is impersonal and goes to work to bring into form the thoughts we have placed upon it.

As a man thinks into the Universal Mind, he sets a law in motion, which is creative, and which contains within Itself a limitless possibility.[31]

All thought is creative, according to the nature, impulse, emotion or conviction behind the thought. Thought creates a mold in the Subjective, into which the idea is accepted and poured, and sets power in motion in accordance with the thought.[32]

In treatment there should always be recognition of the absolute Unity of God and man: the Oneness, inseparability, indivisibility, changelessness, and God as the big circle and man as the little circle. Man is in God and God is man.[33]

---

[31]   The Essential Ernest Holmes, pg 16
[32]   Ibid, pg 23
[33]   Ibid, pg 38

The possibility of demonstration does not depend upon environment, condition, location, personality or opportunity. It depends solely upon our belief, our acceptance and our willingness to comply with the Law through which all good comes. The Universe will never deny us anything, unless we conceive that it is possible for us to think of something that is impossible for the Universe to produce. Everyone who asks receives, according to their belief.[34]

<u>Basis for Spiritual Mind Treatment</u>

Know that God is all there is and that all living things are individualized expressions of the One. We are all united in the One, and all the attributes of the Divine are within each of us now. God expresses Itself through us, as us. It is done unto us as we believe. Practicing the Presence of God puts us in tune with the God within. A way of practicing the Presence is to chant over and over again the following: *"There is only One Life, that Life is God's Life, that Life is Perfect, that Life is my life now."* [35] The key to a powerful treatment is the recognition of the unity of all life with the One Source behind all Creation.

We are Spiritual Beings having a human experience. All

---

[34] The Science of Mind, Ernest Holmes, pg 174
[35] Dr .Robert Henderson, Church of Spiritual Living, Prescott, AZ

healing is done in the Spiritual state of being.

All illness, lack, or other negative emotion is the result of a belief in separation. The reality is that it is impossible to be separate from God. We are all one with the Divine. God knows nothing other than Itself,which is total goodness, love, joy, harmony, wellness, prosperity and oneness with all of Its creation. God is the cause behind all of Its creation and is eternally giving of Itself equally to all.

All Spiritual Mind Treatment is on the mental level and is spiritual rather than physical. We know that from every visible form, there is an invisible counterpart. The general law is that what we are to the Universe, the Universe will be to us; that what we give out, we shall receive back; like attracts like. "It is done unto us as we believe". We are dealing with a Principle, scientifically correct and eternally present, that states we can accomplish whatever it is possible for us to conceive.[36]

We see things as <u>we</u> are, not necessarily as <u>they</u> are. Everything that goes on in our life experience must be interpreted through the filter of our belief system. "Our interpretation of a situation determines whether we will

---

[36]   The Essential Ernest Holmes, pg 15

deem it "good" or "bad."[37] Nothing in of itself is either good or bad—thinking makes it so. Our interpretation of what we see, hear, and feel is what produces our experience. Positive perceptions produce positive experiences.

All Treatment should be done in the first person and in the present moment. The present moment is the only reality. The past is but a trail we have left behind and the future has not occurred. The present moment of now is all that exists.

Practice forgiveness, for that is the way to live in the eternal now. Holding any grudges and perceptions of being hurt or hurting someone else, is denying one's unity with God.

To change our belief and experience, we need only discover the blocking belief and change it with a unifying one to initiate a new cause which the Law will then produce it into form.

The person doing the treatment works to convince him/herself of the Truth of Being. He/she never attempts to change another. The practitioner knows that there is only one Mind, and that we all use this Mind, and to the

---

[37]   The Science of Mind, page 281

extent the one the treatment is for is open and receptive to the truth of his/her being, the remedy will manifest.

Treatment is a definite command: A command to bring into our experience that we desire. We speak our Word with authority, knowing it will be done unto us as we believe and accept.

When treating, all fears and doubts must be relinquished. Accept the truth and declare, "I AM a perfect being and I Am that now".

The process of treatment is to bring into alignment that which we know to be true and that which we are now experiencing.

When one gives a treatment for right action, and does not believe that right action will be the result, he makes his own treatment negative. Therefore, we should spend much time in convincing ourselves of the truth of our treatment. We do not put the power in the treatment;God does that, and we will take out of the treatment only as much as we believe is in it! We do not heal anything. God is the Source and the healing energy in treatment work.

Ernest Holmes offers a suggestion on how often to "treat". "Never let go of the mental image until it

37

becomes manifested. Daily bring up the clear picture of what is wanted and impress it on the mind as an accomplished fact. This impressing on our minds the thought of what we wish to realize will cause our own minds to impress the same thought on Universal Mind. In this way we shall be praying without ceasing."

In treatment work know that Mind is the Actor and you are the director. Think back to Principle, until your thought becomes perfectly clear again. Such is the power of right thinking, that it cancels and erases everything unlike itself. Remember all there really is, is God. Also, God is the Actor and you are the director of your life experience.

There is a divine pattern of perfection behind all creation. We cannot afford to believe in imperfection for a single second, to do so is to doubt God; it is to believe in a power apart from God. Let us daily say to ourselves "Perfect God within me, Perfect Life within me, which is God, come forth into expression through me as that which I am; lead me ever into the paths of perfection and cause me to see only the Good."[38]

Our subjective or unconscious thought patterns can be changed. We have created them and we can change

---

[38]   The Essential Ernest Holmes, pg 56

them. What we put into a treatment will come out of it. Love points the way and Law makes the way possible.

The mind must conceive before the Creative Energy can produce; we must supply the avenue through which It can work. It is ready and willing. It is Its nature to spring into being through our thoughts and action.[39]

If one wants to demonstrate, he must tell himself that he has faith in his power, in his ability, in the Principle and in the certainty of the demonstration for which he works.[40]

The one doing the treating must know, and state that there are no obstacles in the pathway of Truth.

The mental attitude of the one doing the treatment is one of denial toward every false condition that opposes the principle of Life as one of absolute perfection. God's world is perfect and this is the Principle we have to demonstrate. What you are deeply feeling is usually what you are establishing in Mind as cause; it is the pattern for what you will receive.[41]

---

[39] The Essential Ernest Holmes, pg 64
[40] Ibid, pg 65
[41] The Essential Ernest Holmes, pg 78

Remember that it is our belief system that determines how easily and completely the universal goodness flows into our experience. Divine Mind knows nothing of disease, poverty, frustration, or personal estrangement. These conditions are held in place by consistently thinking about them.

There is neither strain nor tension in knowing Divine Truth. Speak your words with authority and a calm knowing, for you are speaking into law through love.

We must accept God as our ONLY SOURCE and trust the perfect expression of the Divine by trusting that our needs are met.

How to give a Spiritual Mind Treatment

The way to give a treatment is first of all to absolutely believe that you can; believe that your word goes forth into a real Creative Power, which at once takes it up, and begins to operate upon it. Feel that to this Power all things are possible.[42]

Ernest Holmes states "All statements used in treatment must be felt with a feeling beyond words, beyond statements and phrases. It is from the essence of this

---

[42] Ibid, pg 58

feeling of Life and Spirit that the mind draws its conclusions, which, presented to the Mind Principle, causes It to react in an affirmative rather than a negative way."

The one doing the Treatment is seeing the Truth (true Nature), in his/her own mind, of the situation he is treating for. His/Her affirmations, declarations, and words are spoken to raise his own consciousness about the situation.

The one doing the treatment cannot know what is going on in the consciousness of the client, as no one can ever know what is in another's consciousness. The one doing the treatment can only know what is in his/her consciousness. Unless you have permission from the client to do treatment work for them, you should never give them a specific treatment. To do so would not be in spiritual integrity. You can always treat for Divine Right Action for their highest and greatest good even if you do not have permission.

Treatment work is for a specific purpose. Before starting a treatment the one doing the treatment must have a specific purpose in mind for what this particular treatment is for. Remember Spirit will never disappoint us when we are absolutely clear about what we want to

41

experience. As Ernest Holmes says "We already are everything we are seeking. What you are looking for, you are looking with."

Treatment work is for a definite purpose. The **Purpose** phase of treatment is the place where you describe what you desire to experience in your life. The purpose should make very clear your intent. Be specific as to what you want to demonstrate and how you'll know when you are demonstrating it. The Spiritual Principle of any Treatment should be also included in the Recognition, Unification, and Realization steps of your treatment.

Religious Science uses Five Steps in Treatment.

- Recognition;
- Unification;
- Realization (of asking and receiving);
- Thanksgiving;
- Release.

Step One: Recognition:

Recognition is the stage where the all-pervading Presence of Spirit is acknowledged and experienced. Treatment is not trying to convince God to do something for you. It is becoming aware of the Presence within you.   It is recognizing that the Life Force and the Source of all creation is the same thing. All problems or ideas of limitation that we perceive stem from a feeling of separation from our Source.

The first thing you do in treatment is to recognize Infinite Spirit— you call to the mind and mentally (verbally if it makes you more comfortable) state, the characteristics of God and the things God does.

•   Example:

"There is Only One Life, One Power, One Divine Energy, One Presence, and One Great Spirit that is infinite and eternal. That Life is here always, ever at work unfolding Its Divine Nature. That Nature is Love, Harmony and absolute Wellness throughout Its Creation."

- **Another Example**:

"God is All there Is. There is One Life and that Life is God's Life and that Life is my life now. God, Creative Intelligence, is continually creating Itself through all of Its creation. God is the Source behind all of Its creation and is eternally giving of Itself to all."

In the Recognition step you align the Divine with whatever the purpose of the treatment is.

Step Two: Unification:

In the Unification step of treatment you start with the identification of God as all there is and unify yourself with God and all Its attributes.

You remind yourself that you are a part of God and that you, too, have all the Infinite Spirit's perfection within you. Your real spiritual self is perfect in every way. You have infinite intelligence and wisdom. Remember, we are the manifest body of God. We are not all that God is, but every cell of our body is God in form. Each of us is a conduit through which the Divine expresses Itself through us as us. You are Spirit in form.

44

Below is an example of the Unification Step of Treatment.

- **Example**:

    I live, move and have my being in the One Life. I am an individualized expression of the Divine. I am that I Am and I know there is that within me that is Perfect, Whole, and Complete. I am united in the One and co-create my life experience.

If you are treating for someone other than yourself, then you should also unify them with God, just as you have done for yourself.

When treating someone else, add the following statement after the example above.

    "What is true about me is also true about John Doe for John is also a unique expression of the Divine and all of God's attributes are within John now."

It should be noted when treating for someone else that the

45

one doing the treatment speaks in third person at all times, always about the client. ("I speak my word for John... I claim for John..."), the one doing the treatment never uses second person pronouns, as though she/he were talking to the client. ("I speak my word for you... I know you are...") The attention of the One doing the treatment should always be directed to God within. To change and direct attention to the client turns a treatment into a conversation. The connection to God as Source is broken, and the power of treatment is diminished.[43]

---

[43] Professional Practitioner Studies, Year II, Term 1, Student Workbook, Class 8, page 5

Step Three: Realization:

This is the step in which you realize how you feel and how things are as you receive that for which you are treating.

In the Realization phase of treatment you build a mental picture of what you desire and imagine how you feel as your desire is fulfilled. Also, realize that your desire is already fulfilled.

All of us find ourselves wanting something at one time or another. Rarely do we take the time to realize that our wanting has two parts to it: the form and the experience of what we want. You and I may both want the same form, such as a new home, but we may want entirely different experiences from having that home. One of the things that makes life seem empty of meaning and fulfillment is when we achieve the form of our desire and it does not bring the experience we wished to have. We are moved away from an empowering relationship with our Source when we go for the form without assessing the experience or qualities of life we are also seeking.

- **Example** 1: Health & Relationships

I know that the perfection of God is continually expressing Itself through me as perfect health, peace, harmony and joyous living. I am open and receptive to the Source of all Good. Through the eternal Givingness of the Divine, I experience perfection within me now. Divine Right Action manifests for my highest and greatest Good now.

- **Example** 2: Health

There is a Divine Pattern of perfection at the very center of my being. Every atom, cell, fiber, organ, muscle of my being works in perfect order right now. I am open and receptive to this Divine pattern and I experience perfect health now. Any thought contrary to this truth of perfection is eliminated forever from my experience.

- **Example** 3: Prosperity

  Through the eternal givingness of the Divine I am
  abundantly supplied with all the money I desire; it
  comes to me at the right time and when I need it.
  All my bills are paid in full; I have plenty of
  money to live a rich and prosperous life now. I am
  prosperous now.

- **Example** 4: Prosperity

  I live in a world that is filled with God's
  abundance, and I now claim this as my own. All
  my affairs are under the law of prosperity.
  Increased good flows to me from all directions
  and through all. I am prosperous in every facet of
  my life. All my needs are met and all my desires
  fulfilled, for I know that I have a loving Spirit
  within that lovingly supplies my every desire now.

- **Example** 5: Employment

  As God is the Source behind all Good, I know
  that I am gainfully employed now. The job I am
  seeking is seeking me now. I am able to utilize my

unique skills to provide service to my fellow man. I know that Divine Right Action results in the prefect job at the right salary and in the perfect time for my highest and greatest good.

Step Four: Thanksgiving:

In this Step you express gratitude and thanksgiving for the fact that omnipotent Spirit is already creating whatever you have treated for. You have a thankful heart and show it. You express thanks for your knowledge of the creative Process and how it works for you.

•   **Example** 1:

"I am grateful for my awareness of the Law and the process of how it works. I am a perfect expression of the Divine now."

•   **Example 2:**

I am grateful for the knowledge that God is the Source of all good and It expresses Itself as prosperity through me now.

.

Step Five: Release:

In this step of the treatment you release your word to the infinite power and intelligence of God's law for demonstration. The Law of Mind is automatic in its action. It creates effortlessly and completely whatever has been accepted in the treatment. You release the treatment and turn from it, secure in the knowledge that your desire is already certain; that as you have accepted it in mind, so will it be manifested in the physical plane.

- Example:

"I release my word into the Law knowing that the work has already been done. I let go and let God. And, so it is."

The Release step in treatment is very important. It is in this step you recognize that you do not do the healing; that it is the Divine within that does the work. By letting go of the treatment and releasing it to the Divine, knowing that the work is already done, you provide the faith, conviction, and belief that the demonstration is at hand.

Here is an analogy to this: let's say you are a farmer who

is preparing the soil for planting his crop. Once he prepares the soil provides the proper fertilizer, and water, he plants the seeds into the field. He fully expects the seeds to grow and prosper without his intervention. He doesn't go out into the field and dig up the seeds to see if they are growing. He trusts that the seeds will grow according to the way they work. That is what is meant when we say Let go and Let God. God is the Actor and we are merely the Director of what direction the Law works.

The above are the five steps of Treatment. They are quite simple and straightforward. Remember, you will not learn these steps unless you start to use them. Once you've started, the more you use them, the better your treatments will become.

Figure 2, is a simple form describing how and what to do in each step of treatment. One might ask how long should a treatment be? The answer is a treatment should be as long or as short as you need in order to arrive at the feeling that you already have what you want; then express your thankfulness and release it to the automatic action of the law of mind for demonstration.

Figure 3 is a Spiritual Mind Treatment worksheet which is to be used in practicing treatment work. I recommend that the student run off copies of this form for their use when doing spiritual mind treatments. Once the student becomes familiar with the steps in treatment and what should be included in each, they will develop their own way of doing treatment work. However, for new students it is recommended that a standard format be used in doing their treatments.

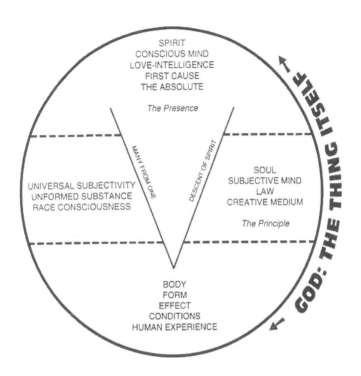

Figure I Metaphysical Chart -- The whole circle represents the totality of Oneness of God (Spirit). In the Top section is Universal Spirit, Love, Absolute, First Cause, and Conscious Mind. The center section is Universal Subjective Mind, Soul, Law, and Creative Medium by which Spirit passes into form. The lower section is the physical manifestation of Spirit— form, effects, or conditions.

SPIRITUAL MIND TREATMENT

A. DEFINE YOUR PURPOSE FOR GIVING A TREATMENT. BE VERY CLEAR ON YOUR INTENT. BE SPECIFIC. WHAT DO YOU WANT TO <u>BECOME</u>? HOW WILL YOU KNOW WHEN YOU "ARE" IT?

EXAMPLE

I WANT TO BECOME A GREATER EXPRESSION OF HARMONY AND PEACE. I WILL KNOW WHEN I HAVE EMBODIED THAT WHEN MY WORK WITH JOE JOHNSON IS PEACEFUL AND HARMONIOUS.

B. 5-STEP TREATMENT

1. RECOGNITION — WHAT IS GOD RELATIVE TO WHAT YOU WANT TO BECOME?

EXAMPLE

"GOD IS INFINITE PEACE AND HARMONY; GOD IS EVERY-WHERE PRESENT"

2. UNIFICATION — WHATEVER YOU KNOW ABOUT GOD IS THE <u>TRUTH</u> OF YOUR BEING.

EXAMPLE

"SINCE GOD IS PEACE AND HARMONY & IS EVERYWHERE PRESENT, THEN GOD'S PEACE & GOD'S HARMONY <u>MUST RESIDE IN ME</u> AND IN <u>ALL HE CREATED.</u>"

COOPERATION · SERENITY · PEACE · HARMONY · ONENESS

3. REALIZATION — TO "MAKE REAL" YOUR DESIRE ... TO CONTEMPLATE HOW THE TRUTH OF YOUR BEING EXPRESSES THROUGH YOU IN YOUR WORLD.

EXAMPLE

"I LET GO OF ANY IDEA OF IN-HARMONY I MAY HAVE HELD IN MIND. NO PAST EXPERIENCE HAS ANY POWER OVER ME.
TODAY PEACE AND HARMONY FLOW THROUGH ME. EVERYTHING I THINK, SAY & DO IS AN EXPRES-SION OF MY DIVINE NATURE. EVERY SITUATION AT WORK IS ESTABLISHED WITH SERENITY & COOPERATION. I SEE JOE JOHN-SON AS GOD'S CREATION WORKING IN A SPIRIT OF HARMONY.
TODAY I AM AT PEACE & I WORK IN HARMONY WITH ALL PEOPLE."

4. THANKSGIVING — AN EXPRESSION OF GRATITUDE.

EXAMPLE

"I GIVE THANKS FOR MY EXPANDED CONSCIOUS-NESS OF HARMONY & PEACE — ESTABLISHED NOW IN MIND."

5. RELEASE — LET GO OF ALL CONCERN—TOTAL ACCEPT-ANCE.

EXAMPLE

"I RELEASE THIS TREATMENT KNOW-ING THE LAW IS CREATING THAT WHICH I HAVE ACCEPTED. MY WORD CANNOT RETURN VOID!"

AND SO IT IS!

Figure 2 - This picture gives an example of each step in doing a Spiritual Mind Treatment, and a brief statement for each, and what should be included in the treatment.

Figure 3 - Spiritual Mind Treatment
Practice worksheet

PURPOSE:

RECOGNITION

UNIFICATION:

REALIZATION:

THANKSGIVING:

RELEASE:

Spiritual Mind Treatment
Practice worksheet

PURPOSE:

RECOGNITION

UNIFICATION:

REALIZATION:

THANKSGIVING:

RELEASE:

Affirmations:

Another tool that goes along with Spiritual Mind Treatments is the use of Affirmations. One should use affirmations to change their belief and the resultant effects from the consequences of wrong thinking. This establishes a new cause of action to manifest their desires in their experience.

I recommend that the student write down affirmations on a 3 x 5 index card and carry them with them; pulling them out and reviewing them any time they experience something other than the Truth of their being. This will greatly facilitate changing their mind and you know that by changing your mind you'll change your experience.

A listing of affirmations that came from United Centers of Spiritual Living daily word is included herein. These are only some of the many affirmations one can use in their daily spiritual practice. I recommend that every one develop their own affirmations. Make it mean something especially to you, for it is your own unique mind that you must change, no others.

Sample Affirmations:

Today, I move within and recognize that there are no limits. A full and overflowing life is mine right now. I rest in the knowledge that I am one with Spirit.

In this moment, I experience the peace of Spirit. I know what is truly important, and I set the intention to live my life from the inside out. I open my heart to all that God offers.

I accept that Spirit is always with me. I am never alone. I choose how I see any situation in my life. I choose to see God, to see growth, and to seek peace.

Right now, I am still and know that I am a powerful co-creator. All my dreams are within my grasp. I see them; I feel them; I live them. I am grateful.

Today, I commit to using my gifts to serve humankind. As I serve, I am both a blessing, and I am blessed.

Today, I release all judgments. I accept that we are all different, yet all divine. I know every time I look into the eyes of another I am seeing God expressing.

In this moment, I open myself to God. I choose to move beyond my comfort zone and step into all I can be. I release all negativity and accept that I am a powerful co-creator with Spirit. I am at peace.

Today, I reach out and tell someone I love them. I make kindness and compassion a regular part of my life.

Today, I see myself as a spiritual being. I realize there are no limits to what I can be or do. I see only my potential to realize and live all my dreams.

In this moment, I recognize that, through my choices, I have the ability to create heaven anywhere I am. I choose heaven and act in every way to bring Spirit into my life and the lives of those I touch.

All the power and presence in the Universe is right where I am. I am always in a state of perfect equilibrium because I am receptive to the divine truth around me and in me.

The intelligence of Spirit expresses through me as right decision and right action. I accept the free flow of life in all of my affairs. I live life to the fullest.

I know that I am filled with joy. I AM experiencing the wonderful love of my creator who delights in giving me this gift. Today I share the joy in my life and I am blessed!

I know the Christ lives within me. I let that bright presence shine. As I share the magnificent gift of love, I make a positive difference in my world. I welcome every opportunity to express the gifts of love and I am blessed.

The power of God within me expresses abundance in wonderful and magnificent ways. My every need is already met. I accept perfect divine action in all of my affairs with gratitude and gladness.

I am a perfect being, living within perfect spiritual conditions. I look for the great and wonderful possibilities in all situations. I release the past and enjoy the beauty and activity of this day.

I give freely and effortlessly to the universe, for that same energy of love and abundance provides for all my needs.

Consciously, I draw upon the Life that is mine. I know that the fullness of life, which is Divine in Its origin, eternal in Its presence, and forever available, is mine. The Life of the eternal Spirit is my Life. The infinite riches of

Its being are mine to enjoy. The vitality, the wisdom, and the peace of God are mine. I accept them in fullness, in joy, and in peace. My thought is a gateway to illumination; it is the secret place of the most High within me. Therefore, I accept the fullness of Life this moment. I accept living as a glorious experience, a spiritual adventure.

Today I uncover the perfection within me. In its fullness I reveal the indwelling kingdom. I look out upon the world of my affairs, knowing that the Spirit within me makes my way both immediate and easy. I know there is nothing in me that could possibly obstruct or withhold the Divine circuit of Life and Love, which Good is. My word dissolves every negative thought or impulse that could throw a shadow over my perfection. Good flows through me to all. Good shines through my thoughts and actions. Good harmonizes my body so that it is revitalized and manifests perfection in every cell, organ and function.

Good harmonizes my mind so that Love sings joyously in my heart. I am in complete unity with Good.

I know that my word penetrates any unbelief in my mind, casts out fear, removes doubt, clears away obstacles, permitting that which is enduring, perfect, and true to be realized. I have complete faith and acceptance that all the statements I make will be carried out as I have believed. I do everything with a sense of reliance upon the Law of Good, therefore I know that my word shall not return unto me void. I accept this word and rejoice in it. I expect complete and perfect results from it.

I believe with a deep, inward calm that my word of faith is the execution of spiritual law in my life. I have absolute reliance upon the Law of Good. I believe that the Law of Good will bring everything desirable into my experience. Today I proclaim my Divine inheritance. I am rich with the Richness of God; I am strong with the Power of God; I am guided by the Wisdom of God. I am held in the goodness of God, today.

I know that every negative condition of the past is swept aside. I refuse to see it or to think about it. Yesterday is no longer here; tomorrow has not yet arrived. Today is God's day. God's day is my day. Today, bright with hope and filled with promise, is mine. I am alive, awake, and aware—today.

I allow the Divine Wholeness to flow through me in ever widening circles of activity. Every good I have experienced is now increased. Every joy that has come into my life is now multiplied. There is a new influx of inspiration into my thought. I see more clearly than ever before that my Divine birthright is freedom, joy, and eternal goodness. The Divine Presence interprets itself to me through love and friendship, through peace and harmony. Knowing that Life gives to me according to my faith, I lift my mind, I elevate my faith, I listen deeply to the song of my being.

Today I realize that my good is at hand. Today I know that my Redeemer liveth in me. He is within me, now, today, this very moment, in this breath I draw, in the eternal now and the everlasting here. The Spirit within me refreshes me. I am saturated with the essence of Life. My mind is an instrument for Its Wisdom; my body, a vehicle for Its Wholeness. Today I shall endeavor to feel this Presence as a living reality in my life. I shall see God everywhere.

I free myself of all false beliefs and awaken this day to the truth of my being. I know the truth and it sets me free.

I allow the infinite abundance of the Universe to flow into my experience today and every day. I contemplate the bounty of God and I accept more and more good into my life.

Today, I release all fear and know that all I need to achieve peace and right action is already mine.

Today, I see the indwelling presence that animates all things. I am a part of the great Energy that is the one source of all being. The One Mind is my mind.

Today, I open myself to be nourished by the beauty in life. My thoughts blossom and bear fruit.

Today I celebrate the pure joy of being alive. I fill my heart with the Divine Presence and live in spontaneous thanksgiving and harmony with all life.

The Mind within me has no limitation in time and space. All that I need comes to me in time and on time from the eternal source.

I realize that the great source of my nourishment is the body of God. All that sustains me comes from the One Life in which I live and have my being.

I live in the Mind of God. I notice every miracle that unfolds before me and give thanks for the gifts of joy and abundance in my life.

Today I am opening my consciousness to a realization of the living Christ, the eternal Sonship of the everlasting Father. I know that He dwells in me and I know that there is an invisible Guide, a living Presence with me at all times. With complete simplicity and directness, I recognize my Divine center. Consciously, I unify myself with this pure Spirit in which I live, move, and have my being. I am strong with the strength of the all-vitalizing Power of pure Spirit. I am sustained by Divine Energy which flows through me as radiant health and vitality. Every atom of my being responds to this Divine Presence. I completely surrender myself to It.

Because my whole being is the Life of God in me, I have nothing to fear. Everyone I meet is part of the same Wholeness in which I live. Every person I meet is a center of the great unity of Life. It is this center of Life that I meet in all persons. It is this unity in and through all that I respond to. I cannot wish anyone harm, nor does anyone desire to harm me. Through my consciousness of love, which is the very essence of goodness, I transform my apparent imperfection into the perfect idea of true being. I know people as God knows them. I am seeing everything as God must see it. His Law is written in my mind and felt in my heart. I see God everywhere.

Nothing enters into my experience but joy, integrity, and friendship. I refuse to hold grudges. All the good I would realize for myself I realize for others as well; I do not deny myself the good I affirm for others. I forgive as I want to be forgiven. I know that in the household in which I live the host is God, the living Spirit Almighty; the guests are all people; the invitation has been eternally written for all to enter and dwell therein in peace and harmony, as the guests of this Eternal Host forever.

I refuse to contemplate evil as a power. I know that it will flee from me; it dissolves and disappears in the light of love. I know that hate cannot exist where love is recognized. I turn the searchlight of Truth upon every apparent evil in my experience. This light dissolves every image of evil. The manifestation of good is complete. Love makes the way clear before me. I am guided into an ever-widening experience of living. My every thought and act is an expression of the goodness which flows from Life.

I know that my search is over. I am consciously aware of the Presence of the Spirit. I have discovered the great Reality. I am awake to the realization of this Presence. There is but one Life. Today I see It reflected in every form, back of every countenance, moving through every act. Knowing that the Divine Presence is in everyone I meet, the Spirit in all people, I salute the good in everyone. I recognize the God-Life responding to me from every person I meet, in every event that transpires, in every circumstance in my experience. I feel the warmth and color of this Divine Presence forevermore pressing against me, forevermore welling up from within me—the wellspring of Eternal Being present yesterday, today, tomorrow, and always.

Knowing that the loving Presence is always closer to me than my very breath, I have nothing to fear. I feel this loving protection around me. I know that the song of Joy, of Love, and of Peace is forever chanting its hymn of praise and beauty at the center of my being; therefore, I tune out of my mind all unhappy and negative ideas. I turn the dial of my thought to the sunshine of life, to brightness and laughter, to the joyous Presence of radiant Spirit. I lay aside all anxiety, all striving, and let the law of Divine Love operate through me into my affairs. Joyfully I anticipate greater abundance, more success, and a deeper peace. Joy wells up within my mind and Life sings Its song of ecstasy in my heart.

I know that the Law of God surrounds me with love and friendship. I let It radiate in my environment, bless everything I touch, make whole that which is weak, turn fear into faith, and accomplish the miracle of healing through love. I welcome the opportunity to love fully, completely, and joyfully. I believe in myself because I believe in God. I accept life fully, completely, without reservation, holding to the conviction that good is the eternal Reality, that God is the everlasting Presence, that

Christ within me is the eternal Guide, that my life is complete today.

I open my spiritual eyes to behold the exquisite nature of Spirit in every person, place and thing. I behold the beauty of God right where I am, wherever I am. I relax and enjoy the fullness of my life.

I no longer tell a negative story about myself. I turn within and I feel the sweetness of Spirit upon me. I rest in the sweetness of my life and give thanks for all of my blessings.

I move from my head to my heart and see others through the eyes of compassion. I let go of my opinions and shine a light of compassion on those whom I may have misjudged. When I perceive the personal choices of others as healing choices I honor myself and free others from my judging mind.

I step out of the getting game and give thanks for everything I have. All that I need is within me and I freely give from the overflow. I am a radiant distribution point of God's good.

I touch the face of God before me. I embrace myself in love and shine that light of love upon every individual I meet. I touch the face of God and I am touched by its holy presence.

I knock on the door of infinite good through the power of my spiritual intention. I set my intention and cultivate the divine qualities of my heart. When the effects of this world distract me, I turn within and begin again.

I open my eyes and behold a rainbow of good everywhere. I accept the infinite hues of life in all their glory! I turn my head around and take in 360 degrees of life!

I am one with the name and the nature of God. My devotion to the name of peace calms my life. I am one with the name and the nature of God and open to receive more good.

I release my limited perceptions about life. I identify with what is spiritually true about me and transcend the limitations I have placed upon myself. I let go of the box of disbelief. I let go of the box of not enough-ness. I let go of the box of self-doubt.

In every moment I consciously choose to turn within and make enlightened choices; by doing so I reveal the intentions of my heart.

Treat, Treat, and Move Your Feet

EXPERENTIAL # 1   Define the Purpose for your treatment

EXPERIENTIAL # 2

List as many of the attributes of God that you can identify

EXPERENTIAL # 3 RECOGNITION

Write a Recognition step of your treatment: bring in the Purpose of your treatment

EXPERENTIAL # 4 UNIFICATION

Write Phrases unifying you with God. Bring into this step the Spiritual Principle relating to your Purpose.

EXPERENTIAL # 5

Write a statement for the Unification Step of Treatment, again including the Purpose.

EXPERENTIAL # 6 REALIZATION

Write a statement for the Realization Step of Treatment. Tie in the Purpose.

EXPERENTIAL #7 THANSKGIVING

Write a Thanksgiving Step of Treatment

EXPERENTIAL # 8 RELEASE

Write a statement for the Release Step of Treatment.

EXPERENTIAL # 9

Write a complete treatment (either a new one or by combining the previous steps in a earlier experiential.

PURPOSE:

RECOGNITION

UNIFICATION:

REALIZATION:

THANKSGIVING:

RELEASE:

NOTES:

NOTES:

NOTES:

NOTES:

Bibliography

FN #   Resource

1. The Science of Mind, Ernest Holmes, Glossary.

2. The Science of Mind, Ernest Holmes, page 149.

3. The Joy of Being, Dr Vetura Papke, page 60

4. The Joy of Being, Dr Vetura Papke, page 63

5. The Science of Mind, Ernest Holmes, page 171

6. The Essential Ernest Holmes, Rev Jesse Jennings, Page, 37

7. The Essential Ernest Holmes, Rev Jesse Jennings, Page 38

8. The Science of Mind, Ernest Holmes, page 203

9. The Science of Mind, Ernest Holmes, page 164

10. The Science of Mind, Ernest Holmes, page 171

11. The Science of Mind, Ernest Holmes, page 170

12. The Science of Mind, Ernest Holmes, pages 63-80
    Living the Science of Mind, Ernest Holmes, pages 1-14, 56-57.

13. Merriam Webster's Collegiate Dictionary

14. The Essential Ernest Holmes, page 192

15. Living the Science of Mind, Ernest Holmes, page 152

16. Can We Talk to God, Effective Prayer, Ernest Holmes, pg 199

17. Can We Talk to God, Effective Prayer, Ernest Holmes, pg 125

18. Living the Science of Mind, Ernest Holmes, page 178

19. The Science of Mind, Ernest Holmes, page 280

20. The Science of Mind, Ernest Holmes, page 280

21. The Mental Equivalent, Emmet Fox, page 5

22. The Mental Equivalent, Emmet Fox, page 7

23. The Mental Equivalent, Emmet Fox, page 24

24. The Essential Ernest Holmes, page 41

25. The Essential Ernest Holmes, page 41

26. The Science of Mind, Ernest Holmes page 413

27. 5 Gifts for an Abundant Life, Diane Harmony, page 21

28. The Essential Ernest Holmes, page 15

29. The Essential Ernest Holmes, page 16

30. The Essential Ernest Holmes, page 23

31. The Essential Ernest Holmes, page 28

32 The Science of Mind, Ernest Holmes, pg 174

33. Dr Robert Henderson, Church of Spiritual Living, Prescott, AZ

34 The Essential Ernest Holmes, page 15

35. The Science of Mind, Ernest Holmes, page 281

36. The Essential Ernest Holmes, page 56

37. The Essential Ernest Holmes, page 64

38. The Essential Ernest Holmes, page 65

39. The Essential Ernest Holmes, page 78

40. The Essential Ernest Holmes, page 58

41. Professional Practitioner Studies, Year, Term I, Student Work Book, Class 8, page 5.

Treat, Treat, and Move Your Feet

Treat, Treat, and Move Your Feet

Made in the USA
San Bernardino, CA
22 November 2015